A NOVICE TIPS FOR A SUCCESSFUL CAREER

A NOVICE TIPS FOR A SUCCESSFUL CAREER

Tried and True Basic Steps

Paul L. Jones

To order additional copies of this book, contact:
Xlibris
844-714-8691
www.Xlibris.com
Orders@Xlibris.com
849555

Contents

Dedication

This book is dedicated to my mother, the late Henrietta S. Jones, and my father, the late Thomas C. Jones. With limited formal education, but with spiritual guidance, good common sense, and hard work, my mother and father taught me, advised me, encouraged me, and provided me, by example, critical life and survival skills.

My mother's formal education was at about the sixth grade level, and my father's formal education was at about the third grade level. However, he did receive some additional education and training through his military service in the US Army. In addition, my mother and father's beliefs and values were strongly anchored in their Christian faith.

With their passing, I realized that a very large part of my drive and passion to achieve success was fueled by a desire to see them succeed, vicariously, through me.

Preface

During my government career, I progressed quite rapidly. I progressed from the entry level to the senior executive level in approximately fifteen years. I consider this a monumental success, especially considering I started this career with what some would say were disadvantages.

My development to adulthood was by austere means and in a monolithic environment. I was the third of six children, born to a couple of very meager means. My first remembrance was of a couple whose husband was recently honorably discharged from the US Army. For most of my formative years, my parents were tenant farmers in eastern North Carolina.

So, as stereotypically depicted, the workday was hard and long. Often, we, the children, had to work on the farm. I don't mean just doing chores, but heavy adult work and not for just an hour or two, but from sunup to sundown. It's hard to image that just twelve years before I started my professional career, I was a ten-year-old working sunup to sundown, doing manual farm labor, plowing or tilling the soil with two mules hitched to a plow, weeding crops, and harvesting crops in the searing hot sun. In several instances, attending school was secondary to work on the farm. In some cases, work was done before and after school. This phase of my life is a whole new book.

There was very little or no pay or profit. And I believe the share[1] was never fair to the tenant. Consequently, there was never any money for extras, such as extra clothes, food, vehicles, or toys.

As with most people, there are things in your past life that one would rather keep secret. This is one part of my life that

---

[1]   Wikipedia defines a **tenant farmer** is one who resides on land owned by a landlord. Tenant farming is an agricultural production system in which landowners contribute their land and often a measure of operating capital and management; while tenant farmers contribute their labor along with at times varying amounts of capital and management. Depending on the contract, tenants can make payments to the owner either of a fixed portion of the product, in cash or in a combination.

I now find difficult to divulge publically. However, I think it's important to reveal for several reasons.

My austere upbringing instilled in me the benefit of hard work and the inspiration and inducement to achieve in order to improve one's status. It also gives me perspective of what hard work means when I hear people today talk about hard work. It also should show those entering the workforce that no matter your circumstances or background, you can succeed.

My monolithic upbringing also did not give me a jump start. In fact, I believe it put me behind the eight ball.

I was raised in a rural, segregated, underprivileged (although, at the time, I didn't realize it), and austere environment. As I stated earlier, I was raised in a rural, segregated environment. For the most part, I had little or no contact with other races, particularly the white race, except for the white folk that owned the farm where we were tenants. I attended all-Black schools from elementary school through college (undergraduate). There was one white student enrolled in the college that I attended. So obviously, I had no sense of the attitude, values, customs, practices, or nuances of other races.

Growing up in this environment, to say the least, I had no idea about the professional work environment or the interworking of professional organizations.

I raise this point not to say I suffered from being raised in this environment. I raise this point to say I didn't have any experiences, advantages, professional knowledge, professional skills, role models, or benefits to jump-start my professional career. While my upbringing environment did not offer me the professional insight to navigating a professional career, it provided me other values, such as the value of hard work, the sense of doing a good job, the desire of getting ahead, the goal of improving one's status, and sense of knowing nothing comes easy. That is, you have to work for what you get.

Acknowledgment

I would like to acknowledge and thank my wife, Hattie, and my sons, Byron and Brenton (deceased while I was writing this book), for the inspiration and support that contributed to my drive to write this book. I would also like to acknowledge my grandson, Brenton Jr., and my granddaughter, Kennedie, and wish them a successful and great future. They all mean the world to me and are one of the reasons I kept going on this project.

Chapter 1

Introduction

"If I only knew then what I know now." "There's no need to rediscover the wheel." "That's tried and true." No doubt you have heard one or more of these quotes or a version of them. Stated simply, each of these quotes means that one had learned a lesson by going through an experience and, in some cases, several experiences or trials and failures. In many cases, a lesson is not learned until one faces failure after several experiences or trials. Some realize failure after going through the same experience several times or doing the same thing but expecting a different result.

There is nothing wrong with learning by experience, but learning this way takes time, and it's not guaranteed to yield a desired result. The result is often counterproductive. If the experience is counterproductive, it often involves a setback.

That is, you have to start all over again or one is farther behind. To clarify, suppose on your job you decide to take a certain approach on a project and the approach results in a negative result. The consequence could be you have to start over, or in the extreme, it could be so detrimental as to cause you to lose your job. Therefore, the lesson learned not only caused you a failure but a setback because you are now out of a job.

So why am I writing this book? I am writing this book to share with you the broad basic lessons and tips that I learned and used to successfully navigate the work environment and climb the promotion ladder. These tips or lessons are the prerequisite to being successful on the job. I want to emphasize that these tips and lessons are the basics. These tips and lessons are the foundation to success. The skills, tricks, and game-playing needed (in addition to the basics described in this book) to get promotions will be described in my next book. Let me clarify. In others words, I am not saying that applying the tips and lessons described in this book will get you promoted. I am saying that these tips are the basic rules of the game. As you know, if you don't play by the rules, you are out of the game. On the other hand, my next book will describe the skills, techniques, and gamesmanship needed to achieve in the game, the tricks of the game, and how to maneuver to be the star of the game.

Hopefully, this book will help you if you are starting out on a new job or career or if you are stuck or not getting promoted on your current job. The idea for this book derived from my encounters with those in the work force who noticed my success and sought my advice on how to succeed.

Basically, I felt inspired or obligated or, shall I say, lead to write this book because I believe that I would be irresponsible or selfish if I did not share my knowledge with those who could benefit from my experiences. In this book, I wish to share my experiences from the prospective of one who was successful in scaling the ladder of success in the workplace.

Hopefully, those entering the job market or are struggling to get ahead in their job will benefit from my experiences and/or tips. I am quite sure that those who find themselves facing a professional career with a background similarly situated as I was will benefit from this book. I sincerely hope they will avail themselves and take advantage of the tips in this book. In addition, I am hopeful that the readers of this book will not have to rediscover the wheel or go through the trials and errors of getting ahead as I did. I believe the tips and experiences in this book will help to jump-start or restart your career. If I had known then (when I started my career) what I know now (what I learned during my career), my career progression would have been more rapid and with less difficulties and indeed "less fits and starts."

Background

I started my career in government at the entry level position and progressed to the senior executive service (SES) level. I had the opportunity to view the operation and management of an agency from every vantage point. Not only was I afforded the opportunity to view the agency from every vantage point, but I also participated in every level of the agency. Therefore, I had the unique opportunity and experience to see and indeed participate in all levels of agency operations. In terms of career progression (from the bottom, the middle, as well as from the upper level) and promotions (from entry level to the SES), this afforded me the unique opportunity to view and discover what it took to get promoted and how decisions on promotions were made.

Having progressed up the chain, I had the opportunity to work with a variety of people and personalities. So not only do I have insights into the technical side of job performance but also insights into the human side of the workforce. In other words, I was involved in the agency core function (accomplishing the agency mission), but also in human resources management (hiring, training, motivating, and promoting its employees).

Like other companies and agencies, the agency where I worked had a pyramid work force. As shown in the figure below, the number of employees at each level of the agencies is the greatest at the bottom of the pyramid. The number of positions shrinks as one progresses to the top to higher levels.

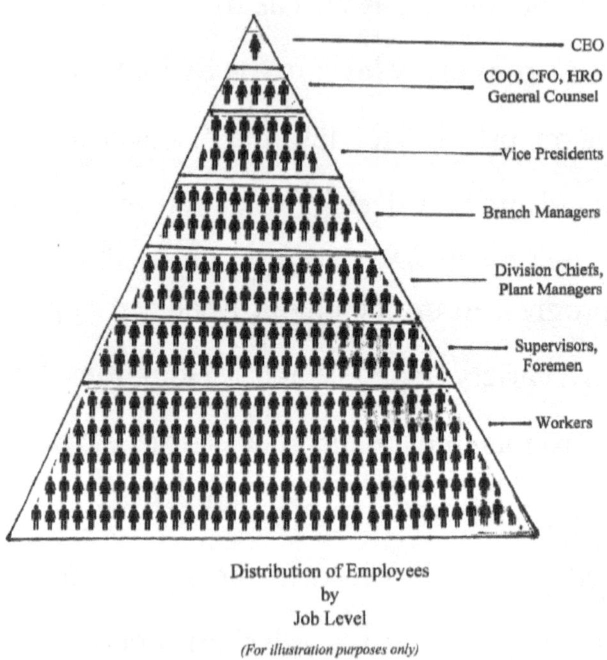

Simply put, competition for positions up the pyramid becomes keener and keener and more intense because there are more qualified and quality employees competing for fewer jobs.

At the entry level, like others at the lower level, I was the low man (person) on the "totem pole," so I did all the low-level jobs and job tasks, including copying, proofreading, "fetching" stuff, etc. Of course, being the low man on the totem pole often meant that I didn't get much respect and/

or opportunity to show what I was capable of doing. Also, being at the bottom, there were incentives to move up the totem pole, such as getting better jobs, answering to fewer people, and receiving more of the benefits—pay increases, recognition and rewards, etc. These benefits come with being at the higher levels of the organization. Also, one key advantage of progression in an organization is there are fewer people to answer to or work for. Not having to respond to or work for some people is a great motivator.

I share my background and experiences with you not to brag or boast but to demonstrate that I have been where you are and have a sense of what you will go through or are going through or have gone through.

The experiences and tips that I will share with you are ones that I have used with proven results. These tips will help you have a successful career and progress steadily in the work force. While I worked at the professional level, I have worked with and indeed was supported by all work levels from paralegals, secretaries, clerks, administration assistants, and mail clerks, to name a few, and I believe these tips apply equally to all levels of the work force. Additionally, while my career was in the federal government, I see no reasons why these experiences and tips would not be applicable to the private sector.

Some of the tips that I am sharing I learned the hard way—from experience or having suffered from violating or not knowing these tips or one of these tips. It would be interesting to share with you how my experiences contributed to discovering these tips, but those experiences are the subject matter of my next book. I will not discuss these experiences at this time. However, in this book I will discuss how the failure to follow these tips can impact or hinder promotions. To amplify why I am writing this book, I have seen a lot of employees who did not advance and wondered why. Often, they tried to relate the failure to get promoted to big things, such as the lack of proper skills or being in the wrong field or job or so forth. However, what I learned by experience and/or by being involved in making promotion decisions is that a lot of employees failed to get promoted not because of the big things but for what to some would seem like little things. If they knew the "real" reason they were not promoted, they would say, "Are you kidding me?" No, I am not kidding. These little things can keep you from getting promoted.

The reason little things prevent an employee from getting promoted is simple—competition. Remember as I said earlier, the competition for promotion gets stiffer as you move up the promotion ladder. There are more employees standing in line for promotion than there are promotions available. So when it comes to competition, the little things can and do make the difference between getting promoted and not getting promoted. The employee who did not get promoted because of one of these little things does not realize that these little things are keeping them from getting promoted.

Even in cases where employees are entitled to feedback on the promotion process, or results, seldom, if ever, is the employee told or given feedback on the "real" reason that he or she did not get promoted. The feedback part of the promotion process encourages feedback based on the job competencies needed to be able to perform at the next level. Normally, performance appraisals are a part of the promotion process. And if an employee is applying for promotion, the performance appraisal(s) will indicate that the employee has performed admirably on his current job indicating that he has the competencies needed for the promotion or to perform at the next job level. If the employee is not promoted often, he is entitled to feedback on why he was not promoted. Normally, the feedback is that the unsuccessful employee did not get promoted because another employee was judged to be a better candidate for the promotion. This is safe feedback, but in most cases, it's not the real reason why the unsuccessful candidate did not get the promotion.

I am calling this safe feedback because it's usually the feedback sanctioned by the agency, it's the feedback that is not confrontational, it's feedback that is not challengeable, and it's the feedback that the employee cannot grieve[2].

---

[2]   As cited at https://www.opm.gov/policy-data-oversight/employee-relations/ employee-rights-appeals/, federal employees have a variety of appeal and grievance rights, depending on the issues involved. Allegations of discrimination, reprisal for whistleblowing, and other prohibited personnel practices can be raised as part of an employee's appeal or grievance.

In February 1969. I entered on duty at the United States General Accounting Office (GAO), now the United States Government Accountability Office.[3]

Thirty-eight years later, in February 2007, I retired from GAO. I started my career at the entry level and retired at the senior executive service (SES) level[4].

When I received a letter of invitation from GAO to come for job interview, I was teaching mathematics at Pomonkey High School in Bryans Road (Charles County), Maryland. My application (SF 171)[5] for employment with the National

---

[3]   The United States General Accounting office, now the United States Government Accountability Office, (GAO) is the independent, non-political, investigative arm of the United States Congress. Its primary function is to review the program and functions of executive agencies and assist the Congress in its oversight of these executive agencies.

[4]   In the United States Government, employees are paid based on a schedule, called General Schedule (GS), with increasing pay corresponding to grades of GS-1 through GS-18. GS grades GS-16 through GS-18 were formally called super grades. More recently, super grades were repositioned and commissioned and renamed the senior executive service. The senior executive service is the highest level of management in the United States' civil service. It's the highest non-appointed position in the US Government.

[5]   The SF 171 (Standard Form 171) is one of the acceptable application forms or documents for Federal employment.

Aeronautics and Space Administration (NASA) had been forwarded to GAO by NASA. I had applied for a position of mathematician at NASA. (I had only applied for a position with NASA because I had heard that a colleague who had graduated ahead of me was working at NASA and was doing pretty good, that is, making pretty good money. When I received GAO's invitation for a job interview, I had not heard of GAO. Nevertheless, as you can surmise, I was offered and accepted GAO's offer of a job as an entry level auditor. I basically accepted GAO's job offer because the salary offered was about 50 percent more than I was making as mathematics teacher. As you can see, I didn't enter GAO with any advantages. I didn't hit the ground running. Additionally, my academic background also did not provide me with any advantages for success at GAO. I had received a BS degree (with honors) in mathematics from Elizabeth City State University. GAO was and is primarily an accounting and auditing agency.

I led many audit teams, including GAO's audits of the US Air Force, and the Department of Defense Military Personnel and Reserve Affairs. Some of the most interesting audits that I performed (I should say led) are the Department of Agriculture meat inspection program, US service academies, gays in the military, use of behavior modification programs in Federal prisons, and homeland security programs.

During phases of my career, I also headed GAO's Office of Program Planning and GAO's Office of Recruitment.

During my career, I worked with three (3) comptroller generals—Elmer Staats, Charles Bowsher, and David Walker. I have met many senior government (federal, state and local) officials and US senators and representatives, written many audit reports, testified before congressional committees several times, and even appeared on television.

As stated earlier, I began my career at GAO at the entry level[6]. I progressed steadily, not necessarily regularly, to

---

[6] Salaries for federal civil service jobs at most agencies are set on the general schedule, or <u>GS pay scale</u>, which links required experience and level of job responsibility to a system of grades and steps within each grade. Grades start at GS-1 and go up to GS-15. Above grade 15 is the senior executive service. As your grade goes up, so does your salary.

the senior executive service (SES)[7] level (I was promoted to and entered the SES in 1987) and retired at the SES level.

In today's job market, it is somewhat unusual to remain at one company or agency for an entire career and indeed unusual to start at the entry level in a company and rise to the senior level management in the company. Today, the phenomenon is an employee jumps from job to job, company to company as he/she gains experience in order to get promoted.

Having progressed from an entry level, GS-7, to the SES, I gained valuable insights, experiences, knowledge, and insider knowledge of what management looks for and considers when making decisions on promotions. I would like to share some of these basic insights into attributes that contribute to getting promoted, hence having a successful career.

---

[7]   In the United States Government, employees are paid based on a schedule, called general schedule (GS), with increasing pay corresponding to grades of GS-1 through GS-18. GS grades GS-16 through GS-18 were formally called super grades. More recently, super grades were repositioned and commissioned and renamed the senior executive ervice. The Senior Executive Service is the highest level of management in the United States civil service. It's the highest non-appointed position in the US Government.

Chapter 2

Appearance/Impression

OK, let's get started. You are getting ready for your first day on the job you have been trying so long and so hard to get, so how do you get started. Start with the obvious. On second thought, let's not assume the obvious. Because for some, the obvious is not the obvious. So how do I decide how basic I should go to explain the obvious?

While in some cases, it may sound like I am stating the obvious, believe me, from my experiences, obvious is not obvious to some. Likewise, what may seem like common sense is not common sense to some. So don't be offended if some of what I am telling you is too basic, and don't feel that I am talking down to you or talking to you in a condescending manner.

Of course, appearance/impression starts at home. And of course, it starts with the obvious, the basics, hygiene—the bath, shave, deodorant, tooth brushing, hairstyle, hair combing, manicure, and fragrances. I know to some this seem obvious, and believe me when I started writing this book, I had no intention of discussing hygiene.

But on reflection, I think there are some out there who need to know this. For others, this maybe not a primer, but a reminder to pay special attention to hygiene. In today's diverse workforce with the diversity of races, ethnicities, cultures, customs, etc., it becomes essential that we pay particular attention to hygiene. Remember, in today's work environment, you are working more and more in teams and near other coworkers. So it's very important that your hygiene is not offensive or in some instances contagious. Also, keep in mind that this is a very sensitive area.

Of all the issues that might surface in the workplace, this one, hygiene, is the one that everyone—friends, coworkers, the supervisors—stays away from mainly because there is so much judgment and not much guidance on what is acceptable and/or allowable. Nevertheless, based on my experience, it's essential that in the workplace that you smell good and look good.

Smell Good

So here are some basic tips on smelling good:

- The bath, take one;
- apply deodorant;
- be careful with the fragrances, including perfumes and colognes (if your fragrance can be smelled before you arrive and lingers after you have gone, you have on too much or it's too strong and overbearing);
- brush your teeth;
- wash and comb your hair, cut the hair where it doesn't belong—out of the nose (this is no place for braids), underarm, etc.; and
- clean and press your clothes. Don't look "lunchy" with food stains all over your clothes.

The Bath

First and foremost, take a bath, head to toe. Don't leave home without it. Use a mild or fragrant-free soap. This is the foundation of smelling good. You are preparing the foundation, which all the other smelling good/looking good parts will be applied.

Don't forget the hair. Shampoo it. This is not just for the fragrance or the smell. Also, for health reasons, it is very important to shampoo your hair. A lot of things can hide in your hair. And some of these things are not good for you or your fellow workers. Again, with the masses of people in the work force, it important that the workplace stays as pleasant and as sterile as possible.

Deodorants

Now that you have taken a bath, it's now time for the deodorant. Go for the antiperspirant and, shall I say, fragrance-free antiperspirant. The use of fragrances is a very sensitive area. My only word of advice is be very careful and use a deodorant with a very mild fragrant, if you use one with a fragrant at all. If for some reason, you prefer not to use a deodorant, I suggest you plan or be prepared to freshen up a time or two while at work. This also brings up the question of the use of colognes and perfumes.

Fragrances

Again, keep in mind that you are working in a closed environment. The environment is very tight, and in many cases, you are working in very close proximity to team members and others in the workplace. There is an infinite number of fragrances on the market. As you know, some of these fragrances, while they might be quite expensive, are very offensive to your olfactory gland or sense of smell. Therefore, it's worthwhile to keep in mind that while your favorite fragrance may smell very, very good to you, its smell my make your team member or a coworker or a fellow worker sick. So keep in mind to make sure that your fragrance has a near neutral a smell as possible or use no cologne or perfume while in the workplace.

I once supervised an employee whose perfume could be smelled before she arrived. And the smell lingered on long after she had left. One of my subordinates (her supervisor) complained to me about her perfume, while at the same time she was complaining to me about his strong, sickening smell of old cigarette smoke and cigarette breath. This smell of cigarette smoke raises the issue of mouth odor, body odor, smell in clothes, etc. (This was back in the day when smoking in the workplace was permitted.) I will get back to this point later.

One of my pet peeves is the person that shakes my hand and the smell of their cologne or perfume lingers on my hand and I can't get it off my hand with soap and water for days.

In addition to fragrances that may have smells that are offensive to team members, coworker and fellow workers; and for whatever reason, some workers are allergic to the ingredients or the smell of some fragrances. While I am not aware of any law or workplace protocol that prohibits the use of fragrances, it would be very considerate if you keep in mind that your fragrance may be offensive and/or make your fellow workers sick.

Oral Care

Your smile is one of your greatest assets. So make sure your smile is pleasant. Smiling usually results in the showing of teeth. Therefore, it's important that when you smile your teeth are presentable and not a turnoff.

For a starter, you should have a complete set of teeth. That is you should have a set of teeth with no visible gaps or missing teeth and no discolored or decayed teeth. I know you are saying it's costly to have dental work to correct blemishes and imperfections in your teeth, particularly when you are starting out in your career. But believe me, it's worth the investment and will pay dividends in the short and long run.

Now that you have a full and complete set of teeth, it's imperative that you keep them white and bright. How do you keep them white and bright? Brush and floss your teeth. Again, keep in mind that you are working in a closed and close environment. During the workday you may also want to brush and floss your teeth, especially after eating lunch or snacks. Brushing your teeth is not just about appearance, but could be a health issue. It is known that bad teeth could lead to catastrophic results.

In addition to brushing and flossing your teeth, keep in mind a related oral issue—bad or offensive breath. During the workday there may be times when you are not be able to brush particularly to remove bad or offensive breath. In these instances, you might need to consider using those products (mouth wash, breath mints, etc.) that mask offensive breath odor.

Look Good

Hair and Nails

Earlier I urged you to shampoo your hair. This was for health and environmental reasons. Now that your hair is clean and odor-free, it's time to consider how it should look. Let me start by saying hairstyles and styling the hair are subjects that probably warrant a separate book, and I won't discuss them here.

However, my overall tip is keeping the hairstyle conservative. This probably would equate to keeping the haircut short, which is also easier to maintain. Today, this could explain why more men, in particular bald men, are opting for shaven heads. This style, if you call it a style, or choice is easier to shampoo and maintain. It also takes less time to get ready for the day. So in summary, keep the style conservative and wash, brush, and comb your hair.

Fingernails

My advice on nails is basically the same as stated for the hair. Keep your nails conservative—clean and short. If you must apply nail polish, keep it as near neutral as possible.

Hands

Believe it or not, your hands make an impression. Imagine you are pointing out something to your boss that is on a printed page. Suppose your nails are long ragged, and your hands are rough, cracked, and not so clean. I would expect that your boss would be somewhat distracted by your hands and not fully focused on what you are showing or explaining. Also, in the workplace, you will always be shaking hands. Your hands should be clean and, to a degree, soft and pleasant to the touch. Lastly, as I stated earlier, refrain from applying moisturizers or other fragrances to your hands that might rub off on others when you shake hands.

Dress for Success

Man, that's an original. Yes, it might sound like a given, but it's just amazing how often we take this tip for granted. As I said before, promotion is a game and you must play the game every day. Don't let your guard down. I know some days, you say, "I don't feel like dressing today," but that will be the day that your boss will ask you to do a presentation to a large group or go to another company to address an issue or to represent him at a very important meeting with some very influential people.

Let me tell you a story. My wife worked for almost twenty-five years as a teacher in the Washington, DC, public schools. It took her a while to realize why she was always being asked by her principal to go to other schools to present workshops on how to teach this or that. She was puzzled because she thought a couple other teachers were better at doing this. And she indeed modeled her teaching techniques after some of these others teachers. She concluded that, after hearing other teachers mumble "she think she's cute," she was sent to other schools to make presentations or represent the principal because her principal felt that she represented the principal well. She was always professional and was professionally well dressed. If you visit our schools today, you will note that some of our teachers dress like the students or as if they will only be seen by students. In some cases, based on their dress, they can't be distinguished from the students. My wife believed that she needed to inspire the student, particularly since the students she taught were primarily from the socioeconomically disadvantaged sections of DC. She wanted to set an example of what is appropriate dress and to show them that dress signifies or helps determine their destiny.

So what is appropriate attire for the workplace? The general answer is, and I don't mean to be flippant, it depends on your job and the culture of your workplace. You are in the best position to determine the appropriate attire for your job.

Usually in government, it's spelled out or you can get clues from your boss and/or your boss's boss. In my career, I worked for a professional, conservative agency. Being a conservative organization, like the big eight accounting firms or law firms, our professional attire was conservative business. This translated into basic standard conservative suits, blue or grey, and dark ties—not brown—and save the black suit for funerals.

I know you are saying, "I am just starting out in my career, I can't afford the proper attire." I am by no means suggesting that you buy the most expensive suits. I have found that in most cases, the lesser cost suits work just as well. However, it might be worth the investment to have your suits properly fitted and tailored. This will add nominally to the cost of your attire, but will leave your attire looking better and you looking better in the attire, and the attire looking more expensive than anyone would imagine

Let me tell you another story. As I said before, you can usually determine what the proper attire is for your job and agency because it's spelled out or by following clues from your boss and/or your boss's boss. In my case, it was more explicit. When I interviewed with GAO, I knew nothing about the agency nor had I even heard about it. I had applied for a job with NASA (National Aeronautical and Space Administration) as a mathematician. I had only applied for the position with NASA merely because I had heard that a former college mate worked for NASA and was doing well—that is, making pretty good money. NASA had forwarded my application to GAO[8]. Toward the end of the interview, the interviewer looked me over (literally) from head to toe and said, "Around here, we wear dark suits and ties. I thought I was snappily dressed. I was wearing

---

[8]   The National Aeronautical and Space Administration (NASA) is the federal government's space agency. When I applied for a job with NASA, it was the civil service's practice that an agency that did not have positions to be filled by an applicant would forward that applicant's applications to other agencies that had jobs to be filled.

a medium brown iridescent suit with a matching tie and brown shoes. I don't think the rules on women dress are quite as explicit as for men. However, when in doubt, error on the conservative side.

As I said before, getting promoted is a game with rules to be followed. If you chose to ignore the rules you could be penalized, which could mean being put out of the game. It is assumed that everyone in the workplace knows the rules. Because of this coworkers and/or friends are afraid or embarrassed, or for selfish reasons, to remind you when you are not properly attired. This reminds me of a specific case where an employee was not informed that her attire was improper, and ultimately, it hurt her. Government, as well as the private sector, is moving toward pay-for-performance. What this means is you are now competing with your coworkers for pay and promotions. Usually, decisions on pay and promotions are made by a panel of upper management.

As an SESer, I sat on these panels and got to see the dynamics of the process. My team was composed of about 150 employees located in Washington, DC, and four regional offices throughout the US, which consisted of all grade levels below the SES. Like the other SESers that served on the annual assessment panel, I did not work with each employee in our team, so we had no personal knowledge of the performance of all employees. However, I like each member of the assessment panel I had to assess the performance of each member of the team in terms of assigning performance pay. As panel members, we also had to assess and rank those employees who applied for promotion. Some of the discussions by the panel were quite interesting and instructive. For example, while trying to describe an employee, a panel member asked, "Is this the woman that wears the prostitute pumps?" Keep in mind, promotion is a game, and this type of comment would tend to kick you out of the game. Yes, your attire does matter, and it is noticed.

I have another story (true) to share with you. As I mentioned before, my wife was a teacher, and occasionally, she would take a needed day of rest and restitution (R and R) leave. On days that my wife would take an R and R day, it was amazing that she would get a call from my son's school to pick up my son because he was not feeling well. It was amazing because on days that she would take R and R, she get up and dress as if she was going to work so our son would not know she was staying home. After this happened several times, my wife asked my son how he knew she would be home. He said, "Mom, there are some things that you do not wear to work, and I notice on days that you were staying home, you would put on clothes, such as pants, that you don't wear to work." This shows that appropriate dress is a must and is noticed.

The advent of business casual in the workplace has relaxed the dress code but added new responsibilities—defining what is appropriate and when it's appropriate to dress casually. One good rule is when in doubt, error on the side of being conservative. When my agency adopted a business casual policy, it issued general guidance on what is appropriate business casual. However, the guidance was quite broad. The policy stated that jeans were not allowed, men could wear sport shirts with the tail tucked in their pants but they had to have a collar, and women were not to wear flip-flops. Employees were left to decide what other specific items were casual, particularly when a specific item was not mentioned in the policy. During a promotion panel discussion, a panel member commented that he had never seen a particular employee's shirt tail tucked in his pants. This comment was made during the panel's deliberations on promotions. How do you think this employee faired in the paneling process?

Extra Clothing

If you work in an agency that allows casual dress, I strongly suggest that you have an extra set of formal clothing available at work just in case you need change clothes to attend a meeting or an event at work that doesn't favor casual attire. As I have discussed the paneling process, it's obvious that you are being judged or evaluated by others in addition to your immediate supervisor. While your immediate supervisor has objective, personal, and first-hand knowledge of your performance, there are numerous persons in the workplace who have opinions of your performance even though they don't work with you and have no direct knowledge of your work. So, it's obvious that their opinion of your work is developed by other means. There impressions are probably derived from how you look and present yourself.

Emergency Kit

It's a good idea to have an emergency kit at work. As you know accidents can and will happen. The emergency kit should contain at least a comb, toothpaste, toothbrush, soap, wash cloth, nail clipper, needle, thread, buttons, and shoe polish. While the need for some of these emergency items may not be apparent, in my experience, there will be times when each one of these items is needed.

I will not give you a scenario where each of these items has been needed. However, there were occasions where each of these items was needed. For example, there will be times when you will spill something on your blouse or shirt or tie, etc. You certainly don't want to attend a key meeting looking "lunchy." There will be times when you lose a button or you have a hang nail, or you had too much garlic on the hoagie for lunch.

Chapter 3

Etiquette (Or Should It Be Image)

One factor that influences other's opinion of your performance is image. Therefore, in addition to dress, another key factor is image. Image is, according to Webster's, a person strikingly like another person. Since image plays a critical part in "outsiders" assessment of your performance, it's important that you project the image that will be conducive to a favorable evaluation. You can project the image that influences "outsiders" assessment of your performance by subscribing to proper office etiquette. I will quickly run through a list of tips on proper office etiquette. Some suggested tips on proper office etiquette are the following:

- Be pleasant. Smile, don't look like you have been sucking on lemons or drinking vinegar. Say "good morning."

- Make conversation with all employees that you encounter, especially with those that can impact your career. Elevators are often quiet zones and create uncomfortable situations because there is limited time to make conversation, and it's all ears. Knowing this, I would prepare scripts that I would recite if I happened to encounter key employees on the elevator or in the hallway. You know who these key people are in your agency, you might want to try this technique. To drive home the importance of this tip, let me tell you another story. During our promotion panel deliberations, the selecting official's comment when discussing a particular employee was "she never speaks to me." How do you think she faired in the process?

- If you can't say something good, don't say anything. Don't say anything negative about fellow employees, office policy, your job, or even the office party. These utterances have a tendency to get back to the wrong people, and often, they are exaggerated and/or embellished, and attributed to you. A corollary of this tip is excuse yourself from negative conversations and environment.

- Be professional. Be about your work. Don't play and don't joke around. Walk with a purposeful gait. Walk like you are going somewhere that's important and you need to be there on time. This gives the impression that you are busy and what you are doing is important.

- Be busy. This probably is a corollary of being professional. You were hired to work, to do a job. So do the job and give the boss a full eight hours of work. I know that in every job there are times when you are not busy, or you feel that you have nothing to do. But here's the tip (trick), keep busy or at least look busy. Let me give you an example. I once worked in what was then called a bull pen. A bull pen is a large open space without any partitions. Everyone had a desk and a workspace, but it was not partitioned off. In the bullpen were about ten auditors, comprised of assistant directors, supervisors, and us staffers. One of my peers had a good reputation for being a hotshot, a very good worker. His supervisor was always praising him and telling all of us how good he was and how hard he worked. It was true that he was a good worker because I had worked with him, but I wasn't sure that he was always busy and productive. At that time, we were noted for writing down all our work on long work sheets called work papers. (This was before computers.) These papers were accumulated into often thick and bulky work paper bundles. I notice that this hotshot was always buried in these work papers and appeared to be always hard at work. I was somewhat puzzled because I was working with him, and admittedly, I wasn't always that busy. So one day, when everyone had gone to lunch, I decided to do some investigative work. I went over to the hotshot's desk and proceeded to go through the work paper bundles that he was always working on. To my surprise, no, I was not surprised. What I discovered was a bunch of crossword puzzles. This hotshot was a crossword puzzle junkie. He was faking being busy by doing crossword puzzles. This issue of being busy takes on a whole new meaning now with the advent of computers, teleworking, and flex time. Now, as it should have been before, workers need to be assessed based on measurable goals and outputs rather than being assessed on being busy or judged based on how hard the worker worked. This brings to mind another coworker who worked late and on weekends and was constantly telling everyone how hard she was working. Later, I had a chance to supervise this employee. It was quite revealing that the reason this employee worked so hard was because she was not a very smart or astute worker. However, viewed from afar, one would conclude that she was a hard worker. Yes, she worked hard because she wasn't very smart.

- Don't loiter around the water cooler. Don't give the impression that you don't have work to do, don't be too social. I know I previously said make conversation. Yes, I did, but you make conversation and move on, don't linger.

- Don't discuss politics, religion, sexual orientation, race, or other controversial subjects like abortion. These conversations can only get you in trouble because no matter what your position, there is an opposing position. I am sure you can recall incidents where noted TV stars lost their jobs for not being political, correct? This could lead to forming unknown enemies that could damage your career.

- Don't be too smart. Don't know everything and/or have an opinion or position on everything. This will make your advice less valuable because you will be seen as shallow or with limited thinking or analytical skills.

- Don't burn bridges. Suppose you need to go back to an office to get some urgently needed information but you have cut your ties with this office, or suppose you need a reference from and employee that you have severed ties with. Don't burn bridges, as you might need to go back across those bridges.

- The boss is right. The boss has the responsibility of the office, as an employee you are merely helping the boss carry out his responsibility. Yes, express your opinion and/or position and make sure your position and/or opinion is understood, but if the boss has a different position, acquiescence. I will discuss this tip in more detail later.

Chapter 4

Infrastructure (Support System)

As I mentioned before your immediate supervisor is the one person who has personal, objective, observed, and firsthand knowledge of your performance. Without your boss's support (good rating, feedback, mentoring, etc.), it's nearly impossible to get promoted.

If you can, or if you can influence the decision, pick your boss. If you can pick a boss, choose one who is respected (one who is seen as objective, truthful, tough but fair, has his boss's ear). The primary objective of the promotion process, the game, is to not get thrown out of the game. Remember the competition for promotion is stiff, so the assessment panel is trying to easily and quickly shorten the list of competitors. One way the panel weighs the competitors is to weight the ratings based on the rater. For example, if a rater is known as an easy rater, the ratings of his subordinates are discounted and questioned. If a rater is known as a tough rater, the tough rater's ratings of subordinated are raised. The adjustment of easy and tough rater's ratings is very subjective and indeed not scientific. The respected rater's ratings are considered at face value.

Get your boss's support of your objective, getting promoted. After all you work for him and are helping him to achieve his work objective. He should be obligated to support you.

Get feedback from your boss. Ask your boss's opinion on what you need to do to get promoted.

Develop a plan for achieving or improving the skills identified by your boss.

Work your plan. Be sure you accomplish or improve on the skills identified by your boss as needing improvement.

Mentors are also a key part of your support system. Ideally, you want to pick mentors that are professionally above you because they have been where you are trying to go so they will have experiences that are very helpful to your success. Mentors should also be able to blaze the path for you because they have more contacts and contacts with employees in higher positions that can influence or have an impact on your career.

While I previously said that it is not wise to discuss religion in the workplace, this does not mean that you should not seek spiritual support.

Chapter 5

Outstanding Performer

You now have the attire, etiquette, and infrastructure. Now, how do you distinguish yourself? Remember promotion is a game. You must find a way to stand out from your competition or be an outstanding performer. You are in competition with your coworkers. The sooner you recognize this fact, the better. Some of these coworkers are peers and, in some cases, even friends. How do you make yourself stand out from your peers and coworkers and be recognized as an outstanding performer?

I don't know your job, so I can't share specifics tasks or jobs technical skills that you need to possess in order to be an outstanding performer. But possessing those technical skills and applying those technical are essential and a prerequisite to being an outstanding performer. However, having a good set of technical skills and applying them well are a necessity; they alone will not get you promoted. Again, you are in competition with your coworkers and peers for promotion. So in order to get ahead or get promoted, you must distinguish yourself from your coworkers or peers.

I would like to share some tips to make you stand out from your coworkers and peers distinguish yourself as an outstanding (promotable) performer. My list of tips is by no means inclusive.

Make the boss's job easy. This is the overarching tip. As an SESer, believe me, we have enough on our plates to worry about. So if you can make the boss's job easier, you are way ahead of the promotion game. So here are the following tips to demonstrating outstanding performance:

- Complete tasks on time.

A product has little or no value if it's not available when needed. Another reason to be timely is because time is one of a handful of measures that can be measured objectively, particularly if you are in a service type of business. Measuring quality is subjective. Timeliness is indisputable; it's measured with a calendar and/or a clock. While I don't have the statistics, I would chance a guess that most disciplinary action are based on timeliness.

Let me share another story with you. I once worked with a difficult employee. He was lazy, not dependable, his work was sloppy, and he needed constant support and guidance. While these attributes are subjective, he made a fatal mistake. He falsified his time card. Unbeknownst to the employee, the check-in scanner recorded check-in time. I once had a mentor who advised me to turn in projects on time, even if incomplete because, as I said earlier, time is measurable quality. It is not debatable and not disputable.

- Do the toughest jobs.

As a GS-13, I took on the challenge of auditing defense contracts that had been awarded sole-source. The objective of the audit was to determine if the government negotiated fair and reasonable prices for these contracts. This was a challenging undertaking. Sole-source contracts are awarded without the advantage of competition to establish a reasonable price. Some of these contracts involve the procurement of large, complex products and services. One of the major contracts that I was responsible for auditing was the government's contract with General Dynamic for the F-16 fighter aircraft. This was a multimillion dollar, multinational contract that included numerous contract changes and numerous subcontracts. Again, the objective of the audit was to determine if the government had negotiated a fair and reasonable contract price based on cost and pricing data used to negotiate the contract price. This was a complicated and taxing assignment, to say the least. But with a team of several auditors from GAO headquarters in Washington, DC, and regional offices in Dallas, Texas, and Dayton, Ohio, the audit was an outstanding success.

The pluses of accepting the toughest jobs are you will have the boss's support, you will get the boss's attention, and the boss will remember and appreciate your efforts. So in essence, the boss won't allow you to fail. There will be too much at stake to let you fail.

- Accept assignments with a smile.

Remember the tip mentioned previously, be pleasant. Think about how you feel when you ask your kids to clean their room or take out the garbage. If they hesitate, frown, mumble, or argue, how do you feel about approaching them the next time these tasks are due. In the workplace, employees who do not accept assignments with a smile are avoided as much and as often as possible. Likewise, when it comes to pay and promotion they are not the first employees considered.

- Support the boss.

This is corollary of the overarching tip, make the boss's job easy. You can support the boss in several ways, for example . . .

> Offer solutions and/or options. Often when you have problem, you have spent more time than the boss trying to resolve the problem. Share your thinking with the boss.

o Volunteer to help others. This saves the boss's time in assigning additional staff.

o The boss is always right. This tip deserves a little discussion. This does not mean that you don't have a position or an opinion. This means that you express your position, make sure your position is understood, and reiterate your position, if needed. However, if the boss rejects your position or adopts another position, after considering your position, drop your position or acquiescence to the boss's position.

Another story. A very junior employee and his supervisor were at loggerhead over a very technical, theoretical, methodology point. Rather than acquiescence to his supervisor's position, the junior employee sought an outside expert who sided with the junior employee's position. The junior employee's supervisor ended up giving in to the junior employee's position. Who do you think won this battle? Let me fast-forward. In the prior appraisal year, the junior employee was on the list of employees identified as best qualified for promotion. During the most recent appraisal year, the junior employee was given an unsatisfactory rating. The junior employee consulted with me when he got the unsatisfactory rating. He did not consult with me when he was at loggerhead with his supervisor.

- Be the go-to person.

The go-to person is the person that the boss can go to perform any task or take on any project. The go-to person is more than likely the person that the boss goes to, to perform sensitive, complex, and/or time critical projects. To be the go-to employee you must exhibit all the attributes described above—do the tough jobs, be pleasant, be timely, and support the boss.

Chapter 6

Understanding the Promotion Process

I should have added another caveat in the beginning—that is, getting promoted is not easy. But I did say there are fewer promotions as you progress up the ladder. The flip side of this caveat is because there are fewer promotions as you move up the ladder, the competition becomes stiffer because more employees are competing for the same position. Before I get to tips on getting promoted or competing for promotions, I believe you need to decide if you want the promotion.

Do you want the promotion? The spontaneous answer is yes. The status would be great. The pay would be great. The psychic income would be great. However, this is a very important decision that requires in-depth and deliberative consideration because each promotion will require changes, such as changes in duties and responsibilities, changes in relationships in both professional and personal, and changes in lifestyle. A promotion could require that you will now have to supervise employees, a task which you do not like. A promotion could mean that you will be required to supervise some close friends, which you would not prefer to do. A promotion could require you to work late hours, including nights and weekends, which would be prohibitive. So it's important that the decision to ask for a promotion or compete for a promotion be very deliberative.

So what are some tips for getting promoted? As I have observed, there are two (2) ways to get promoted: informally competitive and formally competitive. Under the informal process, promotion opportunities are not announced for competition. Individuals are promoted based on demonstrated ability to perform at the next level. It's informal because it's not announced. It's competitive because several employees may be eligible for promotion but only one or a limited number of positions are available. So in a sense, the promotion official has to decide among the eligible employees. Under the informal competitive process, my only tip is ask for promotion.

Another story (true). Early in my career, there came a time when I noticed that other employees, my peers and at my grade level, were getting promoted. After a while, while not getting promoted, I asked my supervisor why I had not been promoted. My supervisor said he did not know I was eligible for promotion. Subsequently I was promoted. So to repeat, under an informal competitive system, ask for promotion.

Let's get to tips under the formal competitive promotion process. I would like to offer the following tips:

- Apply for promotions. The obvious reason for this is if you don't apply, you can't and won't get promoted.
- Take the process seriously. Generally, under the formal competitive promotion process, there is an announcement for promotion (for one or several promotions), which lists performance skills, such as supervision that must be addressed when applying

for the promotion, and timeframes for applying. Address each element of the announcement.

- Follow the process. Adhere to timeframes and deadlines. Don't get thrown out of the game on a technicality.

- Don't get emotional if not successful in the competitive promotion process. If not successful, seek feedback from designated officials and other sources. The designated official will provide feedback, but this feedback might not provide you the real feedback that captures significant comments that were made during the paneling process that are vital to successfully competing for a promotion. What I found amazing, when I sat on panels, was that very, very, very, very few employees approached me about or for feedback on the panel process. Nothing in the regulation, the announcement, or guidance stated or even suggested that this was a prohibited practice.

- Don't get frustrated and opt out of the competitive promotion process. There's a lottery slogan, "You can't win if you don't play." As I said before, because there are numerous employees applying for each promotion, the panel is looking for ways to easily and quickly eliminate employees from the process. Don't make it easy for the panel by not applying.

Chapter 7

You

I have given you some valuable tips on how to get promoted. Use them.

It's now up to **you**

Good luck and God bless you.